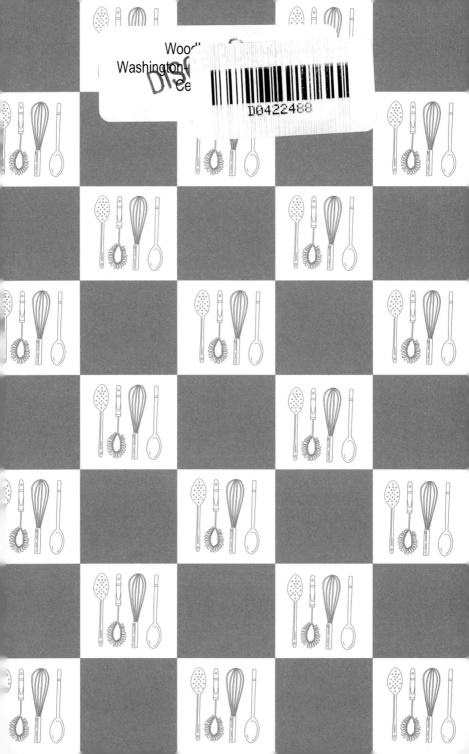

D0422488

.

PERFECT PICNICS

Consultant Editor:
Valerie Ferguson

LORENZ BOOKS

Contents

Introduction

Pack up a picnic and pursue one of life's most delightful pleasures. Despite – or because of – the vagaries of the weather and other uncertainties associated with picnicking, it never fails to be an adventure. Whether you stick a few sandwiches and a couple of apples in a backpack or spread out a banquet by a babbling brook, there's always something special about eating in the open air.

This book will help you plan the perfect picnic from start to finish. There are suggestions for easily transported soups, dips and pâtés; a selection of unusual light bites that can be eaten without cutlery; scrumptious main courses and salads; and wonderful travel-friendly desserts and bakes.

While special equipment is by no means essential, it can make a huge difference to the success of your picnic. Nowadays there is a fabulous array of items available to the dedicated picnicker both for transporting and serving food and drink and for seating the diners comfortably. With all that is on offer to help you, there is no excuse for anything but the most memorable picnic. So relax and enjoy the delicious food and the company – after all, that's the real pleasure of eating out.

Helpful Advice

Transporting Food & Drink

Many types and sizes of lidded food containers are available in rigid plastic which is light and almost unbreakable, some with separate compartments for sauces. Ideally these should be placed inside insulated chiller boxes and bags to keep the food cool. To prevent sogginess, pack oil-based dressings in leakproof lidded containers and shake before adding to salads just prior to serving.

For transporting hot and cold drinks and soup, look for unbreakable steel

Above: Bring a colourful assortment of picnicware which is simply packed away and will not break easily.

flasks, which come in a range of sizes; choose a wide-mouthed flask for soup to make pouring easier. Take mineral water, fruit juices and beer in plastic bottles or cans, which are safer than glass. Wine boxes are a safer option than bottles, and lighter too.

Cakes can be replaced, after cooling, in the tins in which they were baked for transportation.

Tableware

Pack plastic plates and cups. Try to keep utensil requirements to a minimum, concentrating on finger food and items that can be eaten with a fork. Modern picnic tableware is very attractive and there is a wide choice of designs. Bright colours or plain white look best out of doors. It is a good idea to have place settings in individual colours for each guest to make plates and cutlery more easily identifiable.

If you're worried about spilling your wine, buy spiked glasses that stick firmly in the ground.

A picnic hamper looks splendid and is useful for holding chinaware, bottles and utensils, interleaving plates with napkins, and wrapping glasses in dish towels.

Leave the Site As You Found It

Always take care to leave the picnic site as pristine as possible. Make fires only in designated areas and ensure that they are completely extinguished after the picnic. Ensure you take all your litter away with you.

Seating for Comfort

Picnic rugs are pretty, but often too small for a large crowd. An old bedsheet may be more practical, and will certainly be easier to wash. Spread a few large polythene bin or garbage bags underneath it to keep the worst of the damp and dirt at bay, then use the bags for carrying away your rubbish when the picnic is over.

For a large picnic, decorate an old sheet with lots of simple appliqué flower shapes in different colours. Stitch ribbons on the corners and halfway along the sides, then tie these to meat skewers or tent pegs and hammer them into the ground to prevent the cloth flying away.

Take plenty of cushions and back-rests, and pack comfortable garden chairs for older guests.

Equipment Checklist
Plates/bowls
Cups/glasses
Cutlery
Napkins
Corkscrew/bottle opener
Salt and pepper
Kitchen paper
Damp flannels or wipes
Chopping board
Serving spoons and lifters
Knives for food preparation
Picnic rug/cloth
Sunscreen
Insect repellent
Polythene bin bags

Easy Recipes

Summer Punch

A summertime picnic needs a long, cool drink such as this one.

Serves 6 long glasses

INGREDIENTS
several sprigs of fresh borage
¼ cucumber
1 small orange
¼ bottle Pimm's, chilled
several sprigs of fresh mint and/or
    lemon balm
ice cubes
1 bottle lemonade, ginger beer or ginger ale

1 To prepare the flowers, remove each flower-head from the green calyx by gently teasing it out. It should come away easily.

2 Halve the cucumber lengthways, then cut into thin slices. Chop the orange into small chunks. Put in a large transportable lidded jug or pitcher with the slices of cucumber and add the Pimm's, mint, borage sprigs and ice cubes.

3 At the picnic, mix in the lemonade, ginger beer or ginger ale, stirring gently. Serve in tall glasses with flowers on top of each glass.

French Dressing
Makes about 110 ml/3¾ fl oz

INGREDIENTS
90 ml/6 tbsp extra virgin olive oil
15 ml/1 tbsp white wine vinegar
5 ml/1 tsp French mustard
pinch of caster (superfine) sugar

1 Place the olive oil and wine vinegar in a screw-top jar and add the mustard and sugar.

2 Close the jar tightly and shake vigorously. Transport in the jar and shake again before adding to salad.

Scrumptious Sandwiches

Assemble large "sandwiches", such as a *pan bagna,* which is made from a whole baguette, and transport uncut. Wrap closely in greaseproof paper or foil. Divide into portions at the site.

Smoked Salmon & Gravlax Sauce

Mix 25 g/1 oz/2 tbsp butter with 5 ml/1 tsp grated lemon rind and spread over four slices of rye bread. Cover with 115 g/4 oz smoked salmon and add a curly endive leaf and a lemon slice. Spoon over 60 ml/4 tbsp gravlax sauce. Garnish with sprigs of fresh dill.

Parma Ham, Pesto & Mozzarella Cheese

Stir 30 ml/2 tbsp pesto into 60 ml/ 4 tbsp mayonnaise. Use as a filling for bridge rolls, adding sliced Parma ham, mozzarella and vine tomatoes. Include some shredded fresh basil, if you like.

Onion, Spinach & Cheese

Chop an onion and fry in olive oil until golden. Allow to cool. Layer the onion on granary baps with raw spinach leaves and grated Cheddar cheese mixed with mayonnaise.

Crudités

Pack a selection of crisp raw vegetables, cut into slim sticks or strips or broken into florets to serve with dips and pâtés.

Preparing Salad Leaves

1 Wash and drain the leaves. Break off any tough ribs. Dry robust leaves in a salad spinner; blot delicate leaves with kitchen paper.

2 Pack the leaves into polythene bags, close tightly and store in the refrigerator before packing in a chiller bag.

Middle Eastern Yogurt & Cucumber Soup

This refreshing chilled soup is perfect for a hot summer's day.

Serves 4

INGREDIENTS
1 large cucumber, peeled
300 ml/½ pint/1¼ cups single (light) cream
150 ml/¼ pint/⅔ cup plain (all-purpose)
   yogurt
2 garlic cloves, crushed
30 ml/2 tbsp white wine vinegar
15 ml/1 tbsp chopped fresh mint
salt and ground black pepper
fresh mint sprigs, to garnish

1 Grate the cucumber coarsely. Place in a bowl with the cream, yogurt, garlic, vinegar and chopped mint. Stir well and season to taste.

2 Chill for at least 2 hours before serving. Transport in a vacuum flask to keep cool.

3 Just before serving, stir the soup thoroughly. Pour into individual bowls and garnish with mint sprigs.

Sweet Potato & Red Pepper Soup

As colourful as it is good to eat, this soup is a sure winner for picnics.

Serves 6

INGREDIENTS

500 g/1¼ lb sweet potato
2 red (bell) peppers (about 225 g/8 oz), seeded and cubed, plus extra for garnishing
1 onion, roughly chopped
2 large garlic cloves, roughly chopped
300 ml/½ pint/1¼ cups dry white wine
1.2 litres/2 pints/5 cups vegetable or light chicken stock
Tabasco sauce (optional)
salt and ground black pepper
country bread, to serve

1 Peel the sweet potato and cut into cubes. Put in a saucepan with the peppers, onion, garlic, wine and stock. Bring to the boil, lower the heat and simmer for 30 minutes or until all the vegetables are quite soft.

2 Transfer to a blender or food processor and process until smooth. Season with salt, pepper and a generous dash of Tabasco, if liked.

3 Transfer the soup to a vacuum flask if it is to be served warm, though it is also good at room temperature. Garnish with diced red pepper. Serve with country bread.

Spiced Carrot Dip

This sweet and spicy dip makes great picnic fare served with tortilla chips.

Serves 4

INGREDIENTS
1 onion
3 carrots
grated rind and juice of 2 oranges
15 ml/1 tbsp hot curry paste
150 ml/¼ pint/⅔ cup plain (all-purpose) yogurt
1 handful fresh basil leaves
15–30 ml/1–2 tbsp lemon juice
Tabasco sauce
salt and ground black pepper

1 Finely chop the onion. Peel and grate the carrots, setting aside a small quantity for the garnish. Place the onion, carrots, orange rind and juice and curry paste in a small saucepan. Bring to the boil, cover and simmer for 10 minutes until tender.

2 Process the mixture in a blender or food processor until smooth. Leave to cool completely. Stir in the yogurt, then tear the fresh basil leaves into small pieces and stir them into the cooled carrot mixture.

3 Add lemon juice, Tabasco, salt and pepper to taste. Serve within a few hours at room temperature. Garnish with the reserved grated carrot.

Cannellini Bean Dip

A soft bean dip that is good scooped up with wheaten crackers.

Serves 4

INGREDIENTS
400 g/14 oz can cannellini beans
grated rind and juice of 1 lemon
30 ml/2 tbsp olive oil
1 garlic clove, finely chopped
30 ml/2 tbsp chopped fresh parsley
Tabasco sauce
cayenne pepper
salt and freshly ground
   black pepper

1 Drain the beans in a sieve and rinse them well under cold water. Transfer to a shallow bowl.

2 Use a potato masher to roughly purée the beans, then stir in the lemon rind and juice and the olive oil.

3 Stir in the chopped garlic and parsley. Add the Tabasco sauce, cayenne pepper and salt and pepper to taste.

4 Spoon the mixture into a plastic lidded bowl and dust with cayenne pepper. Chill until ready to serve.

VARIATION: Other beans can be used for this dip, for example butter (lima) beans or kidney beans.

Chicken Liver Pâté with Hyssop

Garnished with fresh herb flowers, this rich pâté makes an attractive addition to a picnic spread. Accompany it with a simple tomato or green salad decorated with similar flowers, if you like.

Serves 6–8

INGREDIENTS
50 g/2 oz/4 tbsp butter
115 g/4 oz/⅔ cup bacon, chopped
2 cloves garlic, crushed
1 small onion, finely chopped
450 g/1 lb chicken livers, chopped
60 ml/4 tbsp hyssop flowers and tops, stems removed
60 ml/4 tbsp dry sherry
60 ml/4 tbsp thick double (heavy) cream
5 ml/1 tsp lemon juice
salt and ground black pepper

TO GARNISH
75 g/3 oz/6 tbsp melted butter
1–2 sprigs hyssop flowers and tops

1 Melt the butter in a pan, add the bacon, garlic and onion and cook gently for 4 minutes. Stir in the chicken livers and cook for a further 5 minutes.

2 Add the salt and ground black pepper to taste. Stir in the hyssop flowers and tops and the dry sherry and continue to cook until the liquid has evaporated.

3 Leave the mixture to cool, then blend in a liquidizer or food processor with the thick cream and the lemon juice.

4 Empty the contents into a pâté dish and top with melted butter. Place in the refrigerator overnight to set.

COOK'S TIP: This is an excellent pâté to freeze and enjoy at a later date. Simply place in an airtight container, label, and you'll have an instant and unusual addition to your next picnic.

5 Transport the pâté to the picnic in its dish and serve garnished with sprigs of hyssop in flower.

VARIATION: If you cannot find hyssop, thyme sprigs would make a good alternative.

Mushroom Picker's Pâté

Vegetarian picnickers will love this smooth, intensely flavoured pâté, which will be popular with meat-eaters too.

Serves 4

INGREDIENTS
45 ml/3 tbsp vegetable oil
1 medium onion, chopped
½ celery stick, chopped
350 g/12 oz assorted wild and cultivated
    mushrooms such as closed field
    mushrooms, fairy ring, oyster and
    shiitake mushrooms, bay boletus and
    horn of plenty, trimmed and sliced
150 g/5 oz/⅔ cup red lentils
550 ml/18 fl oz/2½ cups vegetable stock
    or water
1 fresh thyme sprig
50 g/2 oz/4 tbsp almond or cashew
    nut butter
1 garlic clove, crushed
25 g/1 oz bread, crusts removed
75 ml/5 tbsp milk
15 ml/1 tbsp lemon juice
4 egg yolks
celery salt and ground black pepper

1 Preheat the oven to 180°C/350°F/ Gas 4. Heat the oil in a large saucepan, add the onion and celery and brown lightly. Add the mushrooms and soften for 3–4 minutes. Remove a spoonful of the mushroom pieces and set aside.

2 Add the lentils, stock or water and thyme, bring to the boil, uncovered, and simmer for 20 minutes or until the lentils have fallen apart.

3 Place the nut butter, garlic, bread and milk in a food processor and blend until smooth.

4 Add the lemon juice and egg yolks and combine. Add the lentil mixture, blend, then season well with celery salt and pepper. Lastly stir the reserved mushrooms into the mixture.

5 Turn the mixture into a 1.2 litre/ 2 pint/5 cup pâté dish, stand in a roasting tin half filled with boiling water, cover and cook in the oven for 50 minutes. Allow to cool before wrapping in cling film (plastic wrap) and transporting to the picnic.

Cheese Puff Balls

Much easier to make than you might think, these little savoury choux pastries can be eaten plain or stuffed, when cold, with the filling of your choice. Fill on the morning of the picnic.

Serves 4

INGREDIENTS
50 g/2 oz/4 tbsp butter, cubed
1.5 ml/¼ tsp salt
250 ml/8 fl oz/1 cup water
115 g/4 oz/1 cup plain (all-purpose) flour
2 whole eggs, plus 1 yolk
2.5 ml/½ tsp English
    mustard powder
2.5 ml/½ tsp cayenne pepper
50 g/2 oz/½ cup finely grated
    well-flavoured cheese, such
    as Cheddar

3 Return the pan to the heat and beat the mixture, with a wooden spoon, for 1 minute to dry it. Remove the pan from the heat and cool for 5 minutes.

4 Beat in the eggs and yolk, one at a time, then add the mustard, cayenne pepper and grated cheese.

COOK'S TIP: Stir snipped chives, smoked salmon or ham into soft cheese and use as a filling for the puff balls once they are cold.

1 Preheat the oven to 220°C/425°F/ Gas 7. Place the butter, salt and water in a pan. Bring to the boil.

2 Sift the flour on to a sheet of greaseproof (waxed) paper, then, off the heat, tip it all into the butter and water mixture and stir it in very quickly to form a thick paste that leaves the sides of the pan clean.

5 Place teaspoonfuls of the mixture on to a non-stick baking sheet and bake for 10 minutes. Lower the oven temperature to 180°C/350°F/Gas 4 and cook for 15 minutes until well browned. Cool on a wire rack and serve cold. Transport in a sturdy lidded container, spaced apart.

Stuffed Vine Leaves

This vegetarian version of the famous Greek dish uses rice, pine nuts and raisins, and makes excellent picnic food.

Makes about 40

INGREDIENTS
40 fresh vine leaves
60 ml/4 tbsp olive oil
lemon wedges and crisp salad,
    to serve (optional)

FOR THE STUFFING
150 g/5 oz/¾ cup long grain rice, rinsed
2 bunches spring onions (scallions), finely
    chopped
40 g/1½ oz/¼ cup pine nuts
25 g/1 oz/scant ¼ cup seedless raisins
30 ml/2 tbsp chopped fresh
    mint leaves
60 ml/4 tbsp chopped fresh parsley
3.5 ml/¾ tsp ground black pepper
salt

1 Using a knife or a pair of scissors, snip out the thick, coarse stems from the vine leaves. Blanch the leaves in a large pan of boiling salted water until they just begin to change colour. Drain and refresh in cold water.

2 Place all the stuffing ingredients in a large bowl and stir them well to mix together thoroughly.

3 Open out the vine leaves, ribbed side uppermost. Place a heaped teaspoonful of the stuffing on each.

4 Fold over the two outer edges to prevent the stuffing from falling out, then roll up the vine leaf from the stem end to form a neat roll.

5 Arrange the stuffed vine leaves neatly in a steamer and sprinkle over the olive oil. Cook over steam for 50 minutes–1 hour, or until the rice is completely cooked. Serve cold on their own or with lemon wedges and salad if you prefer.

COOK'S TIP: When fresh vine leaves are unavailable, use two packets of vine leaves preserved in brine. Rinse, then drain well before using.

Lemon & Herb Risotto Cake

This unusual rice dish can be served as a main course with salad, or as a satisfying side dish, and packs well for picnics.

Serves 4

INGREDIENTS
1 small leek, thinly sliced
600 ml/1 pint/2½ cups
    chicken stock
225 g/8 oz/1 cup short grain rice
finely grated rind of 1 lemon
30 ml/2 tbsp chopped fresh chives
30 ml/2 tbsp chopped fresh parsley
75 g/3 oz/¾ cup grated
    mozzarella cheese
salt and ground black pepper
fresh parsley sprigs and lemon wedges,
    to garnish

2 Cook the leek in a large pan with 45 ml/3 tbsp of the stock, stirring over a moderate heat, to soften. Add the rice and the remaining stock.

3 Bring to the boil. Cover the pan and simmer gently, stirring occasionally, for about 20 minutes, or until all the liquid is absorbed.

1 Preheat the oven to 200°C/400°F/ Gas 6. Lightly oil a 21 cm/8½ in round, loose-based cake tin (pan).

COOK'S TIP: The best type of rice to choose for this recipe is the Italian round grain Arborio rice, but if it is not available, pudding rice can be used instead.

4 Stir in the lemon rind, chopped fresh herbs, cheese and seasoning. Spoon into the tin, cover with foil and bake for 30–35 minutes or until lightly browned. Turn out and allow to cool. Serve in slices, garnished with parsley and lemon wedges.

Golden Parmesan Chicken

Served with garlicky mayonnaise, these morsels of chicken make mouth-watering picnic fare – they will disappear very quickly!

Serves 4

INGREDIENTS
4 chicken breast fillets, skinned
75 g/3 oz/1½ cups fresh
    white breadcrumbs
40 g/1½ oz/½ cup Parmesan cheese,
    finely grated
30 ml/2 tbsp chopped fresh parsley
2 eggs, beaten
50 g/2 oz/4 tbsp butter, melted
salt and ground black pepper

FOR THE GARLIC MAYONNAISE
100 ml/3½ fl oz/scant ½ cup
    good-quality mayonnaise
100 ml/3½ fl oz/scant ½ cup
    fromage frais
1–2 garlic cloves, crushed

2 Dip the chicken pieces in the egg, then into the breadcrumb mixture. Place in a single layer on a baking sheet and chill for at least 30 minutes.

3 Meanwhile, to make the garlic mayonnaise, mix the mayonnaise together with the fromage frais, garlic and freshly ground black pepper to taste. Spoon the mayonnaise into a small container suitable for transporting to a picnic. Chill until required.

1 Cut each chicken fillet into four or five large chunks. Mix together the breadcrumbs, Parmesan, parsley and seasoning in a shallow dish.

4 Preheat the oven to 180°C/350°F/
Gas 4. Drizzle the melted butter over
the chicken pieces and cook for about
20 minutes, until crisp and golden.
Remove from the oven and allow to
cool before putting into a
transportable container. Serve with the
garlic mayonnaise for dipping.

25

Chicken Lollipops

These tasty stuffed wings will be a great hit with picnickers. As their name implies, they are easy to eat, simply held in the hand.

Makes 12

INGREDIENTS
12 large chicken wings
oil, for deep frying

FOR THE FILLING
5 ml/1 tsp cornflour
1.5 ml/¼ tsp salt
2.5 ml/½ tsp fresh thyme
pinch of ground black pepper

FOR THE COATING
225 g/8 oz/generous 3 cups
   dried breadcrumbs
30 ml/2 tbsp sesame seeds
2 eggs, beaten

1 Remove the wing tips and discard or use them for making stock. Skin the second joint sections, removing the two small bones, and reserve the meat for the filling.

2 Mince the reserved meat and place in a bowl. Add all the filling ingredients and mix thoroughly.

3 Holding the large end of the bone on the third section of the wing and using a sharp knife, cut the skin and flesh away from the bone, scraping down and pulling the meat over the small end to form a pocket. Repeat with the remaining wing sections.

4 Fill the tiny meat pockets with the prepared filling. To make the coating, mix the dried breadcrumbs and the sesame seeds together. Place the breadcrumb mixture and the beaten egg in two separate dishes.

5 Brush the filled meat pockets with beaten egg and roll in the breadcrumb mixture to cover. Chill and then repeat the process to give a second layer of breadcrumbs, forming a thick coating. Chill until ready to fry.

6 Preheat the oven to 180°C/350°F/ Gas 4. Heat 5 cm/2 in oil in a heavy-based pan until hot but not smoking or the breadcrumbs will burn. Gently fry two or three lollipops at a time until golden brown, remove and drain on kitchen paper. Complete cooking in the oven for 15–20 minutes until cooked through. Remove from the oven and leave to cool.

Fennel & Lavender Tarts

Fragrant lavender combines perfectly with the aromatic flavour of fennel.
These mouth-watering tartlets make an appealing addition to any picnic.

Serves 4

INGREDIENTS
115 g/4 oz/1 cup plain (all-purpose) flour
pinch of salt
50 g/2 oz/4 tbsp chilled butter,
    cut into cubes
10 ml/2 tsp cold water
fresh lavender flowers,
    to garnish

FOR THE FILLING
75 g/3 oz/6 tbsp butter
1 large Spanish onion, finely sliced
1 fennel bulb, trimmed and sliced
30 ml/2 tbsp fresh lavender flowers
    or 15 ml/1 tbsp dried culinary lavender,
    roughly chopped
2 egg yolks
150 ml/¼ pint/⅔ cup crème fraîche
salt and ground black pepper

1 Sift the flour and salt together. Rub
the butter into the flour until the
mixture resembles breadcrumbs. Stir in
the water and bring the dough
together to form a ball.

COOK'S TIP: You might find it
easier and quicker to make the
pastry in a food processor.

2 Roll out on a lightly floured
surface to line four 7.5 cm/3 in,
round, loose-based flan tins. Prick the
bases with a fork and chill.

3 Preheat the oven to 200°C/400°F/
Gas 6. To make the filling, melt the
butter in a pan. Add the onion, fennel
and lavender. Reduce the heat. Cover
with wet greaseproof paper and cook
for 15 minutes until golden.

4 Line the pastry cases with baking
parchment and bake blind for
5 minutes. Remove the paper and
bake for 4 minutes more. Reduce the
temperature to 180°C/350°F/Gas 4.

5 Mix the egg yolks, crème fraîche
and seasoning together. Spoon the
onion mixture into the pastry cases.
Spoon the crème fraîche mixture on
top and bake for 10–15 minutes until
set, puffed up and golden. Allow to
cool, then garnish with lavender
flowers before serving.

Marinated Fish

With a number of sharp flavours, this is a strong, zesty dish – just the thing for *al fresco* eating. Serve with cold beer, if you like.

Serves 6–8

INGREDIENTS
1.75 kg/4–4½ lb tuna, carp or pike steaks
75 g/3 oz/6 tbsp butter, melted
50 ml/2 fl oz/¼ cup dry sherry
salt and ground black pepper

FOR THE MARINADE
400 ml/14 fl oz/1⅔ cups water
150 ml/¼ pint/⅔ cup wine vinegar
150 ml/¼ pint/⅔ cup good fish stock
1 onion, thinly sliced
6 white peppercorns
2.5 ml/½ tsp ground allspice
2 cloves
1 bay leaf
25 ml/1½ tbsp bottled capers,
    drained and chopped
2 dill pickles, diced
120 ml/4 fl oz/½ cup olive oil
green salad, dill pickles and pumpernickel
    or rye bread, to serve

1 Preheat the oven to 180°C/350°F/ Gas 4. Put the fish steaks into an ovenproof dish and brush with the butter. Sprinkle over the sherry. Season well and bake for 20–25 minutes or until just tender. Leave to cool.

COOK'S TIP: Look out for capers preserved in salt, which have a superior flavour to those in vinegar.

2 Meanwhile, to make the marinade, boil the water, vinegar, fish stock, onion, spices and bay leaf together in a pan for 20 minutes. Leave to cool before adding the capers, dill pickles and olive oil.

3 Once the fish steaks have cooked, pour over the marinade. Cover the dish with clear film (plastic wrap).

4 Place the dish in the refrigerator and leave for 24 hours to marinate the fish, basting occasionally. Transport in a plastic lidded container and serve with green salad, dill pickles and slices of pumpernickel or rye bread.

Crispy Spring Chickens

These succulent small birds are basted with a honey-flavoured glaze and roasted until the skin is crisp and golden brown.

Serves 4

INGREDIENTS
2 x 900 g/2 lb chickens
salad and lime wedges, to serve

FOR THE HONEY GLAZE
30 ml/2 tbsp clear honey
30 ml/2 tbsp sherry
15 ml/1 tbsp vinegar
salt and ground black pepper

2 To make the honey glaze, mix the honey, sherry and vinegar together. Brush the glaze evenly over the birds. Season generously with salt and freshly ground black pepper.

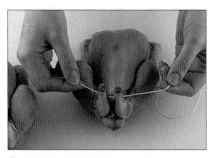

1 Preheat the oven to 180°C/350°F/ Gas 4. Tie the birds into a neat shape and place on a wire rack over the sink. Pour over boiling water to plump the flesh, then pat dry with kitchen paper.

COOK'S TIP: Halve and joint the chickens before packing them in the picnic basket to make serving and eating easy.

3 Place the rack in a large roasting tin and cook the birds in the oven for 45–55 minutes. Baste well with the honey glaze until they are crisp and golden brown.

4 Remove the roasted chickens from the oven and allow them to cool. Wrap in cling film (plastic wrap) and serve cold with salad and lime wedges.

COOK'S TIP: The honey glaze could also be used when roasting ready-prepared chicken pieces such as thighs or drumsticks.

33

Game Pie with Port

A good game pie is one of the triumphs of the traditional picnic hamper.

Serves 8–10

INGREDIENTS
450 g/1 lb/4 cups plain (all-purpose) flour
10 ml/2 tsp salt
175 g/6 oz/¾ cup lard or white vegetable fat
175 ml/6 fl oz/¾ cup milk, or milk
    and water
beaten egg, to glaze
10 ml/2 tsp powdered gelatine
30 ml/2 tbsp cold water
salt and freshly ground black pepper
mixed salad, to serve

FOR THE FILLING
675 g/1½ lb lean boneless game, such as
    pheasant, grouse, partridge and
    rabbit, diced
115 g/4 oz rindless streaky (fatty) bacon
    rashers, chopped
115 g/4 oz/½ cup minced (ground) pork
30 ml/2 tbsp port
10 ml/2 tsp grated orange rind
2 juniper berries, crushed
2.5 ml/½ tsp dried sage

1 Preheat the oven to 200°C/400°F/
Gas 6. Sift the flour and salt into a
bowl and make a well in the centre.

2 In a pan, bring the lard or vegetable
fat and milk or milk and water to the
boil. Pour into the well in the flour
and mix until cool enough to handle.
Knead until smooth, then wrap in
clear film and leave to cool.

3 To make the filling, mix all the
ingredients in a bowl. Season with
plenty of salt and pepper.

4 Roll out two-thirds of the dough
and use it to line a 20 cm/8 in
springform cake tin (pan). Do not trim
the edge of the pastry.

5 Fill the pastry case with the meat
mixture. Brush the edge of the pastry
with beaten egg. Cover the pie with
the remaining pastry, making a hole
in the middle. Trim and crimp the
edge. Decorate the lid with pastry
shapes cut from the trimmings.

6 Bake the pie for 30 minutes, then lower the oven temperature to 180°C/350°F/Gas 4 and bake for 1¼ hours, covering the pie with foil if it starts to over-brown. After 1 hour, remove the sides of the tin. Quickly brush the sides of the pie with beaten egg and return it to the oven.

7 Sprinkle the gelatine over the water in a heatproof bowl. When spongy, stir over simmering water until dissolved. Pour through a funnel into the pie and leave to cool. Transport to the picnic in a sturdy lidded container and serve the pie in generous slices, with plenty of mixed salad.

San Antonio Tortilla

This thick, baked omelette, densely packed with succulent vegetables, travels well and tastes delicious.

Serves 4

INGREDIENTS
15 ml/1 tbsp vegetable oil
½ onion, sliced
1 small green (bell) pepper, seeded
    and sliced
1 garlic clove, crushed
1 tomato, chopped
6 black olives, pitted and chopped
3 small potatoes (about 275 g/10 oz),
    cooked and sliced
50 g/2 oz sliced chorizo sausage,
    cut into strips
15 ml/1 tbsp chopped canned jalapeño
    peppers, or to taste
50 g/2 oz/½ cup Cheddar
    cheese, grated
6 extra-large eggs
45 ml/3 tbsp milk
2.5–3.5 ml/½–¾ tsp salt
1.5 ml/¼ tsp ground cumin
1.5 ml/¼ tsp dried oregano
1.5 ml/¼ tsp paprika
ground black pepper
fresh parsley sprigs,
    to garnish

VARIATION: To serve this dish
to vegetarians simply omit the
chorizo sausage.

1 Preheat the oven to 190°C/375°F/ Gas 5. Heat the oil in a non-stick frying pan. Add the onion, green pepper, and garlic and cook over medium heat for 5–8 minutes until the onion and pepper have softened.

2 Transfer the vegetables to a 23 cm/ 9 in round, non-stick cake tin (pan). Add the tomato, olives, potatoes, chorizo and jalapeños. Sprinkle with the cheese and set aside.

3 In a bowl, combine the eggs and milk and whisk until frothy. Add the salt, cumin, oregano, paprika and black pepper to taste. Whisk to blend.

4 Pour the egg mixture into the vegetable mixture, tilting the pan to spread it evenly. Bake for about 30 minutes until set and lightly golden. Allow to cool and transport in a sturdy lidded container. Serve cut into wedges, garnished with parsley.

Mediterranean Quiche

The strong flavours of tomatoes, peppers and anchovies, beautifully complemented by the cheesy pastry in this unusual quiche, taste even better in the open air.

Serves 12

INGREDIENTS
225 g/8 oz/2 cups plain (all-purpose) flour
pinch of salt
pinch of mustard powder
115 g/4 oz/½ cup butter, chilled
   and cubed
50 g/2 oz/½ cup Gruyère cheese, grated

FOR THE FILLING
50 g/2 oz can anchovies
   in oil, drained
50 ml/2 fl oz/¼ cup milk
30 ml/2 tbsp French mustard
45 ml/3 tbsp olive oil
2 large Spanish onions, sliced
1 red (bell) pepper, seeded and very
   finely sliced
3 egg yolks
350 ml/12 fl oz/1½ cups double (heavy)
   cream
1 garlic clove, crushed
175 g/6 oz/1½ cups mature Cheddar
   cheese, grated
2 large tomatoes, thickly sliced
salt and ground black pepper
30 ml/2 tbsp chopped fresh basil,
   to garnish

1 Place the flour, salt and mustard powder in a food processor. Add the butter and process the mixture until it resembles breadcrumbs.

2 Add the Gruyère cheese and process again briefly. Add enough iced water to make a stiff dough: it will be ready when the dough forms a ball. Wrap the dough in clear film (plastic wrap) and chill for 30 minutes.

3 Meanwhile, to make the filling, soak the anchovies in the milk for 20 minutes. Drain away the milk.

4 Roll out the chilled pastry and line a 23 cm/9 in loose-based flan tin (pan). Spread over the French mustard and chill for a further 15 minutes. Preheat the oven to 200°C/400°F/Gas 6.

5 Heat the oil in a frying pan and cook the onions and red pepper until soft. In a separate bowl, beat the egg yolks, cream, garlic and Cheddar cheese together; season well with salt and freshly ground black pepper.

6 Arrange the tomatoes in a single layer in the pastry case. Top with the onions and pepper and the anchovies. Pour over the egg mixture. Bake for 30–35 minutes. Allow to cool and garnish with the basil before serving.

Mushroom Boreg

This version of a Turkish *boreg*, or pastry parcel, makes an unusual picnic dish, popular with vegetarians.

Serves 4

INGREDIENTS

50 g/2 oz/⅓ cup couscous
45 ml/3 tbsp olive oil
1 medium onion, chopped
225 g/8 oz assorted wild and cultivated
   mushrooms, trimmed and sliced
1 garlic clove, crushed
60 ml/4 tbsp chopped fresh parsley
5 ml/1 tsp chopped fresh thyme
1 egg, hard-boiled and shelled
salt and ground black pepper

FOR THE YOGURT SAUCE

200 ml/7 fl oz/scant 1 cup plain (all-purpose)
   yogurt
45 ml/3 tbsp chopped fresh mint
2.5 ml/½ tsp caster (superfine) sugar
1.5 ml/¼ tsp cayenne pepper
1.5 ml/¼ tsp celery salt
a little milk or water
1 fresh mint sprig, to garnish

FOR THE BOREG PASTRY

400 g/14 oz/3½ cups self-raising (self-rising)
   flour
5 ml/1 tsp salt
1 egg, plus extra for glazing
150 ml/¼ pint/⅔ cup plain (all-purpose)
   yogurt
150 ml/¼ pint/⅔ cup olive oil
grated rind of ½ lemon

1 Preheat the oven to 190°C/375°F/Gas 5. Just cover the couscous with boiling water and soak for 10 minutes or until the liquid is absorbed.

2 Heat the oil in a pan and gently fry the onion for a few minutes to soften without letting it colour. Add the mushrooms and garlic and cook until the juices begin to run. Increase the heat to evaporate the juices. Transfer to a bowl, add the parsley, thyme and couscous and stir well. Grate the hard-boiled egg into the mixture, season and combine.

3 To make the sauce, blend the yogurt with the mint, sugar, cayenne pepper and celery salt, adjusting the consistency with a little milk or water as necessary. Chill until required.

4 To make the pastry, sift the flour and salt into a bowl. Make a well in the centre, add the egg, yogurt, oil and lemon rind and combine with a knife.

5 Turn on to a floured surface and roll into a 30 cm/12 in circle. Pile the couscous mixture into the centre and bring the edges over to enclose. Turn upside down on a baking sheet and press flat. Glaze with egg and bake for 25 minutes. Garnish the sauce with mint and serve with the *boreg*.

Salad Niçoise

This Provençal salad, with its well-defined flavours, makes unbeatable summer outdoor food. Serve it with country-style bread and a bottle of refreshing, chilled white wine.

Serves 4

INGREDIENTS
115 g/4 oz green beans, trimmed
115 g/4 oz mixed salad leaves
½ small cucumber, thinly sliced
4 ripe tomatoes, quartered
200 g/7 oz can tuna in oil, drained
50 g/2 oz can anchovies, drained
4 eggs, hard-boiled
½ bunch radishes, trimmed
50 g/2 oz/⅓ cup small
    black olives
fresh flat-leaf parsley, to garnish

FOR THE DRESSING
90 ml/6 tbsp extra virgin olive oil
2 garlic cloves, crushed
15 ml/1 tbsp white wine vinegar
salt and freshly ground black pepper

1 To make the dressing, whisk together the olive oil, garlic and white wine vinegar and season to taste with salt and freshly ground black pepper.

2 Halve the green beans and cook in a saucepan of boiling water for 2 minutes until they are only just tender, then drain.

3 Mix the salad leaves, cucumber, tomatoes and beans in a large, shallow salad bowl. Flake the tuna. Halve the anchovies lengthways. Shell and quarter the eggs.

4 Scatter the radishes, drained tuna, anchovies, hard-boiled eggs and olives over the salad. Pour over the dressing and toss together lightly. Serve garnished with parsley.

Fennel & Orange Salad

Ideal with spicy or rich foods.

Serves 4

INGREDIENTS
2 oranges
1 fennel bulb
115 g/4 oz rocket (arugula) leaves
50 g/2 oz/⅓ cup black olives

FOR THE DRESSING
30 ml/2 tbsp extra virgin olive oil
15 ml/1 tbsp balsamic vinegar
1 small garlic clove, crushed
salt and ground black pepper

1 With a vegetable peeler, cut strips of rind from the oranges, leaving the pith behind, and cut into thin julienne strips. Cook in boiling water for a few minutes. Drain. Peel the oranges, removing all the white pith. Slice them into thin rounds and discard any seeds.

2 Halve the fennel lengthways and thinly slice across the bulb, preferably in a food processor fitted with a slicing disc or using a mandoline. Combine with the oranges in a bowl and toss with the rocket.

3 To make the dressing, mix together the oil, vinegar, garlic and seasoning. Pour over the salad, toss and leave to stand briefly. Sprinkle with the olives and strips of orange rind.

Aubergine & Caper Salad

Delicious with cold meats or pasta.

Serves 4

INGREDIENTS
1 large aubergine (eggplant), about 675 g/ 1½ lb
60 ml/4 tbsp olive oil
grated rind and juice of 1 lemon
30 ml/2 tbsp capers, rinsed
12 pitted green olives
30 ml/2 tbsp chopped fresh flat-leaf parsley
salt and ground black pepper

1 Cut the aubergine into 2.5 cm/1 in cubes. Heat the oil in a large frying pan and cook the aubergine cubes over a medium heat for about 10 minutes, tossing regularly, until golden. You may need to do two batches. Drain on kitchen paper and sprinkle with salt.

2 Place the aubergine cubes in a large serving bowl, toss with the lemon rind and juice, capers, olives and chopped parsley. Season well. Serve cold.

COOK'S TIPS: This tastes even better made a day in advance. Store, covered, in the refrigerator. Add toasted pine nuts and shavings of Parmesan cheese to serve.

Right: Fennel & Orange Salad (top);
Aubergine & Caper Salad

Tabbouleh Salad

This tasty salad actually improves if it is made a day in advance.

Serves 4–6

INGREDIENTS
225 g/8 oz/1⅓ cups bulgur wheat
15 cm/6 in piece cucumber
2 tomatoes
3–4 spring onions (scallions)
about 60 ml/4 tbsp chopped fresh mint
about 90 ml/6 tbsp finely chopped
    fresh parsley
75 ml/5 tbsp olive oil
30 ml/2 tbsp lemon juice
salt and ground black pepper

1 Cover the bulgur wheat with water and leave to soak in a bowl for about 30 minutes. Drain it thoroughly through a fine sieve.

2 Peel and dice the cucumber. Peel the tomatoes by soaking for a minute in boiling water: the skins will then slip off easily. Chop the flesh into small pieces, discarding the seeds. Slice the spring onions.

3 Mix the drained wheat with the vegetables and herbs. Whisk the oil with the lemon juice and seasoning and stir into the wheat. Chill until required.

Right: Tabbouleh Salad (top); Roasted Pepper Salad (bottom).

Roasted Pepper Salad

This colourful salad is an eye-catching addition to a picnic spread.

Serves 6–10

INGREDIENTS
6 (bell) peppers, in mixed colours
90–120 ml/6–8 tbsp olive oil
salt and ground black pepper

1 Preheat the oven to 190°C/375°F/ Gas 5. Halve the peppers, discarding the seeds and membranes, and cut them into 2.5 cm/1 in strips.

2 Pour half of the oil into a roasting tin (pan) and put the tin into the oven for a few minutes to heat. Arrange the peppers in a single layer in the tin, turning them to make sure they are well coated with oil. Season generously and drizzle over the remaining oil.

3 Roast the peppers in the oven for 20–30 minutes, moving them around once so that those near the edges of the tin don't brown more than those in the centre.

4 Turn the peppers out on to a large plate and leave to cool slightly. With a sharp knife peel off the charred skin. Allow to cool completely. To serve, arrange the peppers in groups of red, yellow and green on a decorative dish.

Potato Salad

Use either new or waxy potatoes for this classic East European salad, since they will hold their shape when cooked.

Serves 6

INGREDIENTS
675 g/1½ lb potatoes
45 ml/3 tbsp olive oil
4 smoked streaky (fatty) bacon slices,
    rinded and chopped
10 ml/2 tsp lemon juice
2 celery sticks, chopped
2 pickled sour cucumbers,
    diced
5 ml/1 tsp German mustard
45 ml/3 tbsp mayonnaise
30 ml/2 tbsp snipped fresh chives,
    plus extra to garnish
15 ml/1 tbsp chopped fresh dill,
    plus extra to garnish
salt and ground black pepper
lettuce leaves, to serve

1 Cook the unpeeled potatoes in a pan of boiling salted water for 15 minutes, until just tender. Drain, allow to cool for 5 minutes, then slice thickly and set aside in a bowl.

COOK'S TIP: German mustard is typically dark with a medium heat and a slightly sweet flavour; it is an ideal accompaniment for sausages, ham and bacon.

2 Meanwhile, heat 15 ml/1 tbsp of the oil in a frying pan and fry the bacon for 5 minutes until crisp. Remove the bacon and set aside.

3 Stir the remaining oil and lemon juice into the pan, then pour over the sliced warm potatoes. Add the celery, cucumber and half the bacon and mix well. Leave to cool.

4 Blend the mustard in a small bowl with the mayonnaise, herbs and a little seasoning. Add to the salad and toss well to coat. Sprinkle with the remaining bacon, garnish with herbs and serve with lettuce leaves.

Dried Fruit & Nut Coleslaw

A delicious and nutritious mixture tossed in a light mayonnaise dressing.

Serves 6

INGREDIENTS
225 g/8 oz white cabbage
1 large carrot
175 g/6 oz/¾ cup ready-to-eat
    dried apricots
50 g/2 oz/½ cup walnuts
50 g/2 oz/½ cup hazelnuts
115 g/4 oz/¾ cup raisins
30 ml/2 tbsp chopped fresh parsley or
    chives or a mixture
105 ml/7 tbsp mayonnaise
75 ml/5 tbsp plain (all-purpose)
    yogurt
salt and ground black pepper
chopped fresh chives, to garnish

1 Shred the cabbage, coarsely grate the carrot and place both in a mixing bowl. Roughly chop the apricots and nuts. Stir them into the cabbage and carrots with the raisins and herbs.

2 In a separate bowl, mix together the mayonnaise and yogurt and season to taste. Add the mayonnaise to the cabbage mixture and toss together to mix and coat thoroughly.

3 Cover the bowl and set aside for at least 30 minutes before serving, to allow the flavours to mingle. Serve the coleslaw garnished with a few chopped fresh chives.

Late Summer Salad with Nasturtiums

This stunningly beautiful salad will bring gasps of delight from picnickers.

Serves 4–6

INGREDIENTS
about 16 young nasturtium leaves
mixed salad leaves
2–3 cooked beetroot (beet)
about 16 whole nasturtium flowers,
    stems removed
about 4–6 nasturtium flower buds

FOR THE DRESSING
4 crushed nasturtium seeds
60 ml/4 tbsp walnut or olive oil
10 ml/2 tsp white wine or
    balsamic vinegar
salt and ground black pepper

1 Create an outer wall of young nasturtium leaves around the edge of a deep salad bowl. Add an inner wall of mixed salad leaves.

2 Slice the beetroot very thinly and place in layers between the mixed salad leaves and the nasturtium leaves. Decorate with nasturtium flowers and buds, reserving a whole flower to place in the centre.

3 Mix together the dressing ingredients in a lidded container and transport separately. Pour over the salad just before serving.

Lemon Cheesecake with Forest Fruits

A luscious, creamy dessert that is guaranteed to delight the eyes as well as the appetites of picnickers.

Serves 8

INGREDIENTS
50 g/2 oz/4 tbsp unsalted butter
25 g/1 oz/2 tbsp light soft brown sugar
45 ml/3 tbsp golden (light corn) syrup
115 g/4 oz/generous 1 cup cornflakes
10 g/¼ oz sachet powdered gelatine
225 g/8 oz/1 cup cream cheese
150 g/5 oz/generous ½ cup Greek (US-strained) yogurt
150 ml/¼ pint/⅔ cup single (light) cream
finely grated rind and juice of 2 lemons
75 g/3 oz/scant ½ cup caster (superfine) sugar
2 eggs, separated
225 g/8 oz/2 cups mixed, prepared fresh forest fruits, such as blackberries, raspberries and redcurrants, to decorate
icing (confectioners') sugar, for dusting

1 Place the butter, brown sugar and syrup in a saucepan and stir over a low heat until the mixture has melted and is well blended. Remove from the heat and stir in the cornflakes.

2 Press the mixture over the base of a deep, 20 cm/8 in, loose-based, round cake tin. Chill for 30 minutes.

3 Sprinkle the gelatine over 45 ml/3 tbsp water in a bowl and leave to soak for a few minutes. Place the bowl over a pan of simmering water and stir until the gelatine has dissolved.

4 Place the cheese, yogurt, cream, lemon rind and juice, caster sugar and egg yolks in a large bowl and beat until smooth and thoroughly mixed.

5 Add the hot gelatine to the cheese and lemon mixture and beat until well mixed. Whisk the egg whites until stiff, then fold into the cheese mixture.

6 Pour the cheese mixture over the cornflake base and gently level the surface. Chill for 4–5 hours until the filling has set. Decorate the cheesecake with the mixed fresh fruits just before leaving for the picnic and dust with icing sugar. Transport in a lidded container and serve in slices.

French Apple Tart

For added flavour, toasted, flaked almonds are scattered over the top of this classic tart, which transports well.

Serves 8

INGREDIENTS
115 g/4 oz/½ cup unsalted butter, softened
50 g/2 oz/4 tbsp vanilla sugar
1 egg
225 g/8 oz/2 cups plain (all-purpose) flour

FOR THE FILLING
50 g/2 oz/4 tbsp unsalted butter
5 large tart apples, peeled, cored
  and sliced
juice of ½ lemon
300 ml/½ pint/1¼ cups double (heavy) cream
2 egg yolks
25 g/1 oz/2 tbsp vanilla sugar
50 g/2 oz/½ cup ground
  almonds, toasted
25 g/1 oz/2 tbsp flaked almonds, toasted,
  to garnish

1 Place the softened butter and vanilla sugar in a food processor and process them well together. Add the egg and process to mix it in well.

2 Add the flour and process until you have a soft dough. Wrap in clear film (plastic wrap) and chill for 30 minutes.

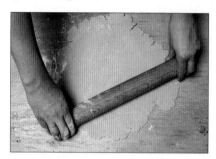

3 Roll out the pastry on a lightly floured surface to about 23–25 cm/ 9–10 in diameter. Line a flan tin with the pastry and chill it for a further 30 minutes.

4 Preheat the oven to 220°C/425°F/ Gas 7 and place a baking sheet in the oven to heat up. Line the pastry case with baking parchment and baking beans and bake blind on the baking sheet for 10 minutes. Then remove the beans and paper and cook for a further 5 minutes.

5 Turn the oven down to 190°C/ 375°F/Gas 5. To make the filling, melt the butter in a large frying pan and lightly sauté the apples for 5–7 minutes. Sprinkle the apples with lemon juice.

6 Beat the cream and egg yolks with the sugar. Stir in the toasted ground almonds. Arrange the apple slices on top of the warm pastry and pour over the cream mixture.

7 Bake for 25 minutes or until the cream is just about set – it tastes better if the cream is still slightly runny in the centre. Transport in its tin and serve cold, scattered with flaked almonds.

Lemon Roulade with Lemon Curd Cream

This featherlight roulade with a rich lemon filling makes a marvellous dessert for a picnic treat.

Serves 8

INGREDIENTS

4 eggs, separated
115 g/4 oz/½ cup caster (superfine) sugar
finely grated rind of 2 lemons
5 ml/1 tsp pure vanilla extract
25 g/1 oz/¼ cup ground almonds
40 g/1½ oz/⅓ cup plain (all-purpose) flour, sifted
45 ml/3 tbsp icing (confectioners') sugar, for dusting

FOR THE LEMON CURD CREAM
300 ml/½ pint/1¼ cups double (heavy) cream
60 ml/4 tbsp ready-made lemon curd

1 Preheat the oven to 190°C/375°F/ Gas 5. Grease a 33 x 23 cm/13 x 9 in Swiss roll tin (pan) and line with baking parchment.

2 In a bowl, beat the egg yolks with half the caster sugar until foamy. Beat in the lemon rind and vanilla extract, then fold in the almonds and flour.

3 Whisk the egg whites until they form stiff, glossy peaks. Gradually whisk in the remaining caster sugar to form a stiff meringue. Stir half the meringue mixture into the egg yolk mixture and fold in the rest.

4 Pour into the prepared tin (pan), level the surface and bake for 10 minutes or until risen and spongy to the touch. Cover loosely with a sheet of baking parchment and a damp dish towel. Leave to cool in the tin.

5 To make the lemon cream, whip the cream, then lightly fold in the lemon curd. Sift the icing sugar over a piece of non-stick baking parchment. Turn the sponge out on to it. Peel off the lining paper and spread the lemon curd cream over the sponge, leaving a border around the edge.

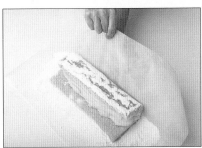

6 Using the paper underneath as a guide, roll up the sponge from one of the long sides. Keep the roulade wrapped to transport it and remove the paper wrapping just before serving. Cut into slices.

Moist Orange & Almond Cake

A versatile cake that is easy to transport to the picnic site, this can be eaten plain or made more luxurious with the suggested accompaniments.

Serves 8

INGREDIENTS
1 large orange
3 eggs
225 g/8 oz/generous 1 cup
    caster (superfine) sugar
5 ml/1 tsp baking powder
225 g/8 oz/2 cups ground almonds
25 g/1 oz/¼ cup plain (all-purpose) flour
icing (confectioners') sugar, for dusting
whipped cream and orange slices,
    to serve (optional)

1 Wash the orange and pierce it with a skewer. Put it in a deep saucepan and pour over water to cover completely. Bring to the boil, lower the heat, cover and simmer for 1 hour or until the skin is very soft. Drain, then cool.

2 Preheat the oven to 180°C/350°F/ Gas 4. Grease a 20 cm/8 in, round cake tin (pan) and line it with baking parchment. Halve the orange and discard the pips. Place it, skin and all, in a blender or food processor and purée until smooth and pulpy.

3 In a bowl, whisk the eggs and caster sugar until thick. Fold in the baking powder, ground almonds and flour. Fold in the orange purée.

4 Pour into the prepared tin, level the surface and bake for 1 hour or until a skewer inserted into the middle comes out clean. Cool the cake in the tin for 10 minutes, then turn out on to a wire rack, peel off the lining paper and allow to cool completely.

5 Dust the top liberally with icing sugar and serve, with whipped cream if you wish. For added colour, tuck thick orange slices under the cake just before serving.

COOK'S TIPS: It is vital to cook the orange slowly first, so it is fully tender before being blended. Don't use a microwave to speed things up – this makes orange skin tough.
  For a treat, serve the cake with spiced poached kumquats.

Mini Focaccia with Pine Nuts

Pine nuts add little bites of nutty texture to these Italian-style small breads, which make great outdoor eating.

Makes 4 mini loaves

INGREDIENTS
350 g/12 oz/3 cups plain (all-purpose) flour
2.5 ml/½ tsp salt
10 ml/2 tsp easy-blend (rapid rise) dried
 yeast
about 250 ml/8 fl oz/1 cup lukewarm water
45 ml/3 tbsp olive oil
45–60 ml/3–4 tbsp pine nuts
10 ml/2 tsp coarse sea salt

1 Sift the flour and salt into a mixing bowl. Stir in the yeast, make a well in the centre of the dry ingredients, and pour in the water and 30 ml/2 tbsp of the oil. Mix well, adding more water if the mixture seems dry. Turn on to a floured surface and knead for 10 minutes until smooth and elastic.

2 Place the dough in a greased bowl, cover and leave in a warm place for about 1 hour until doubled in size. Knock back and knead the dough for 2–3 minutes.

3 Divide the dough into four equal pieces. Take each piece in turn and pat out, using your hands, so that it forms an oblong measuring about 10 x 7.5 cm/4 x 3 in and rounded at the ends. Place on lightly greased baking sheets.

4 Scatter over the pine nuts and gently press them into the surface of the dough. Sprinkle with coarse sea salt and brush with the remaining olive oil. Cover the loaves with greased clear film (plastic wrap) and leave them to rise for about 30 minutes.

5 Preheat the oven to 220°C/425°F/
Gas 7. Remove the clear film and
bake the focaccia for 15–20 minutes
until golden. Cool on a wire rack
before serving.

VARIATION: For a change, try
varying the toppings for these mini
focaccia. Fresh rosemary, sun-dried
tomatoes and Parmesan cheese all
work well.

Petal & Seed Bread

Sunflower seeds are frequently added to breads and rolls. Here, the petals are included as well. To make an interesting coloured loaf you can add a few strands of saffron.

Makes 1 x 500 g/1¼ lb loaf

INGREDIENTS
½ sachet saffron (optional)
50 g/2 oz/scant ½ cup
  sunflower seeds
275 g/10 oz packet white
  bread mix
15 ml/1 tbsp mustard seeds or
  onion seeds
5 ml/1 tsp curry powder
petals of 1 sunflower
salt and ground black pepper
milk, to glaze

1 If using, put the saffron in a small bowl with 30 ml/2 tbsp boiling water and leave for 5 minutes. Heat the sunflower seeds in a dry frying pan for approximately 3–4 minutes until the seeds are just beginning to colour. Leave to cool.

COOK'S TIP: A simple method of making sunflower baguettes is to take ready-prepared dough and place the sunflower petals over the surface of the dough before rolling up and baking in the oven. The flavouring from the petals is scrumptiously nutty.

2 Put the bread mix in a bowl with the saffron and liquid and add all but 30 ml/2 tbsp of the sunflower seeds, the mustard or onion seeds, curry powder and a little seasoning. Pull the petals from the sunflower and add to the bowl. Add 175 ml/6 fl oz/¾ cup hand-hot water and mix to a dough.

3 Turn out on to a floured surface and knead gently for 5 minutes.

VARIATION: This tasty bread is just as good made without sunflower petals if they are unavailable.

4 Place in a lightly oiled 500 g/1¼ lb loaf tin and cover loosely with oiled clear film. Leave in a warm place until the dough has risen well above the top of the tin. Preheat the oven to 220°C/425°F/Gas 7.

5 Brush the top of the loaf lightly with milk. Score diagonally several times and sprinkle with the remaining sunflower seeds. Bake for 15 minutes until turning golden, then reduce the temperature to 180°C/350°F/Gas 4 and bake for a further 15 minutes. Turn out of the tin and leave to cool on a wire rack.

Index

This edition is published by Lorenz Books,
an imprint of Anness Publishing Ltd,
108 Great Russell Street, London WC1B 3NA info@anness.com

www.lorenzbooks.com; www.annesspublishing.com

© Anness Publishing Limited 2014

If you like the images in this book and would like to investigate
using them for publishing, promotions or advertising, please visit
our website www.practicalpictures.com for more information.

Publisher: Joanna Lorenz
Editor: Valerie Ferguson & Helen Sudell
Series Designer: Bobbie Colgate Stone
Designer: Andrew Heath
Production Controller: Steve Lang

Recipes contributed by: Catherine Atkinson,
Kathy Brown, Carla Capalbo, Lesley Chamberlain,
Trisha Davies, Michelle Derriedale-Johnson,
Joanna Farrow, Christine France, Silvano Franco,
Shirley Gill, Judy Jackson, Carole Handslip,
Norma MacMillan, Sue Maggs, Maggie Mayhew,
Norma Miller, Anne Sheasby, Liz Trigg,
Laura Washburn, Steven Wheeler, Polly Wreford.

Photography: Karl Adamson, Edward Allwright,
James Duncan, Ian Garlick, Michelle Garrett,
Amanda Heywood, David Jordan, William Lingwood, Patrick
McLeavey, Debbie Patterson.

A CIP catalogue record for this book is available from the
British Library

COOK'S NOTES

Bracketed terms are intended for American readers.

For all recipes, quantities are given in both metric and imperial
measures and, where appropriate, in standard cups and spoons.
Follow one set of measures, but not a mixture, because they are
not interchangeable.

Standard spoon and cup measures are level. 1 tsp = 5ml, 1 tbsp =
15ml, 1 cup = 250ml/8fl oz. Australian standard tablespoons are
20ml. Australian readers should use 3 tsp
in place of 1 tbsp for measuring small quantities.

American pints are 16fl oz/2 cups. American readers should use
20fl oz/2.5 cups in place of 1 pint when measuring liquids.

Electric oven temperatures in this book are for conventional
ovens. When using a fan oven, the temperature will probably
need to be reduced by about 10–20°C/20–40°F. Since ovens
vary, you should check with your manufacturer's instruction
book for guidance.

Medium (US large) eggs are used unless otherwise stated.

PUBLISHER'S NOTE: